APPLE COMES WITH WHICH LETTER OF THE ALPHABET?
CORRECT ANSWER HERE YOU GO!!

HAPPY TREE !
HAPPY TREE !
I WANT APPLES !
A
FOR APPLE

BANANA COMES WITH WHICH LETTER OF THE ALPHABET?
CORRECT ANSWER HERE YOU GO!!

HAPPY TREE !
HAPPY TREE !
I WANT BANANAS !
B
FOR BANANA

CHERRY COMES WITH WHICH LETTER OF THE ALPHABET?
CORRECT ANSWER HERE YOU GO!!

HAPPY TREE !
HAPPY TREE !
I WANT CHERRIES !
C
FOR CHERRY

THE DATE COMES WITH WHICH LETTER OF THE ALPHABET?
CORRECT ANSWER HERE YOU GO!!

HAPPY TREE !
HAPPY TREE !
I WANT DATES !
D
FOR DATE

ELDERBERRY COMES WITH WHICH LETTER OF THE ALPHABET?
CORRECT ANSWER HERE YOU GO!!

HAPPY TREE !
HAPPY TREE !
I WANT
ELDERBERRIES !
E
FOR ELDERBERRY

FEIJOA COMES WITH WHICH LETTER OF THE ALPHABET?
CORRECT ANSWER HERE YOU GO!!

HAPPY TREE !
HAPPY TREE !
I WANT FEIJOAS !
F
FOR FEIJOA

GRAPE COMES WITH WHICH LETTER OF THE ALPHABET?
CORRECT ANSWER HERE YOU GO!!

HAPPY TREE !
HAPPY TREE !
I WANT GRAPES !

G
FOR GRAPE

HONEYDEW COMES WITH WHICH LETTER OF THE ALPHABET?
CORRECT ANSWER HERE YOU GO!!

HAPPY TREE !
HAPPY TREE !
I WANT
HONEYDEWS!
H
FOR HONEYDEW

ITA PALM COMES WITH WHICH LETTER OF THE ALPHABET?
CORRECT ANSWER HERE YOU GO!!

HAPPY TREE !
HAPPY TREE !
I WANT ITA PALMS !
I
FOR ITA PALM

JACKFRUIT COMES WITH WHICH LETTER OF THE ALPHABET?
CORRECT ANSWER HERE YOU GO!!

HAPPY TREE !
HAPPY TREE !
I WANT JACKFRUITS
!
J
FOR JACKFRUIT

KUMQUAT COMES WITH WHICH LETTER OF THE ALPHABET?
CORRECT ANSWER HERE YOU GO!!

HAPPY TREE !
HAPPY TREE !
I WANT KUMQUATS !
K
FOR KUMQUAT

LEMON COMES WITH WHICH LETTER OF THE ALPHABET?
CORRECT ANSWER HERE YOU GO!!

HAPPY TREE !
HAPPY TREE !
I WANT LEMONS !
L
FOR LEMON

MANGO COMES WITH WHICH LETTER OF THE ALPHABET?
CORRECT ANSWER HERE YOU GO!!

HAPPY TREE !
HAPPY TREE !
I WANT MANGOS!
M
FOR MANGO

NECTARINE COMES WITH WHICH LETTER OF THE ALPHABET?
CORRECT ANSWER HERE YOU GO!!

HAPPY TREE !
HAPPY TREE !
I WANT NECTARINES !
N
FOR NECTARINE

ORANGE COMES WITH WHICH LETTER OF THE ALPHABET?
CORRECT ANSWER HERE YOU GO!!

HAPPY TREE !
HAPPY TREE !
I WANT ORANGES
O
FOR ORANGE

PINEAPPLE COMES WITH WHICH LETTER OF THE ALPHABET?
CORRECT ANSWER HERE YOU GO!!

HAPPY TREE !
HAPPY TREE !
I WANT PINEAPPLES !
P
FOR PINEAPPLE

QUINCE COMES WITH WHICH LETTER OF THE ALPHABET?
CORRECT ANSWER HERE YOU GO!!

HAPPY TREE !
HAPPY TREE !
I WANT QUINCES !
Q
FOR QUINCE

RASPBERRY COMES WITH WHICH LETTER OF THE ALPHABET?
CORRECT ANSWER HERE YOU GO!!

HAPPY TREE !
HAPPY TREE !
I WANT RASPBERRIES !
R
FOR RASPBERRY

STRAWBERRY COMES WITH WHICH LETTER OF THE ALPHABET?
CORRECT ANSWER HERE YOU GO!!

HAPPY TREE !
HAPPY TREE !
I WANT STRAWBERRIES!
S
FOR STRAWBERRY

TOMATO COMES WITH WHICH LETTER OF THE ALPHABET?
CORRECT ANSWER HERE YOU GO!!

HAPPY TREE !
HAPPY TREE !
I WANT TOMATOES !
T
FOR TOMATO

GNI COMES WITH WHICH LETTER OF THE ALPHABET?
CORRECT ANSWER HERE YOU GO!!

HAPPY TREE !
HAPPY TREE !
I WANT UGNIS !
U
FOR UGNI

VELVET TAMARIND COMES WITH WHICH LETTER OF THE ALPHABET?
CORRECT ANSWER HERE YOU GO!!

HAPPY TREE !
HAPPY TREE !
I WANT VELVET TAMARINDS
V
FOR VELVET TAMARIND

WATERMELON COMES WITH WHICH LETTER OF THE ALPHABET?
CORRECT ANSWER HERE YOU GO!!

HAPPY TREE !
HAPPY TREE !
I WANT
WATERMELONS !
W
FOR WATERMELON

XIMENIA COMES WITH WHICH LETTER OF THE ALPHABET?
CORRECT ANSWER HERE YOU GO!!

HAPPY TREE !
HAPPY TREE !
I WANT XIMENIAS !
X
FOR XIMENIA

YANGMEI COMES WITH WHICH LETTER OF THE ALPHABET?
CORRECT ANSWER HERE YOU GO!!

HAPPY TREE !
HAPPY TREE !
I WANT YANGMEIS !
Y
FOR YANGMEI

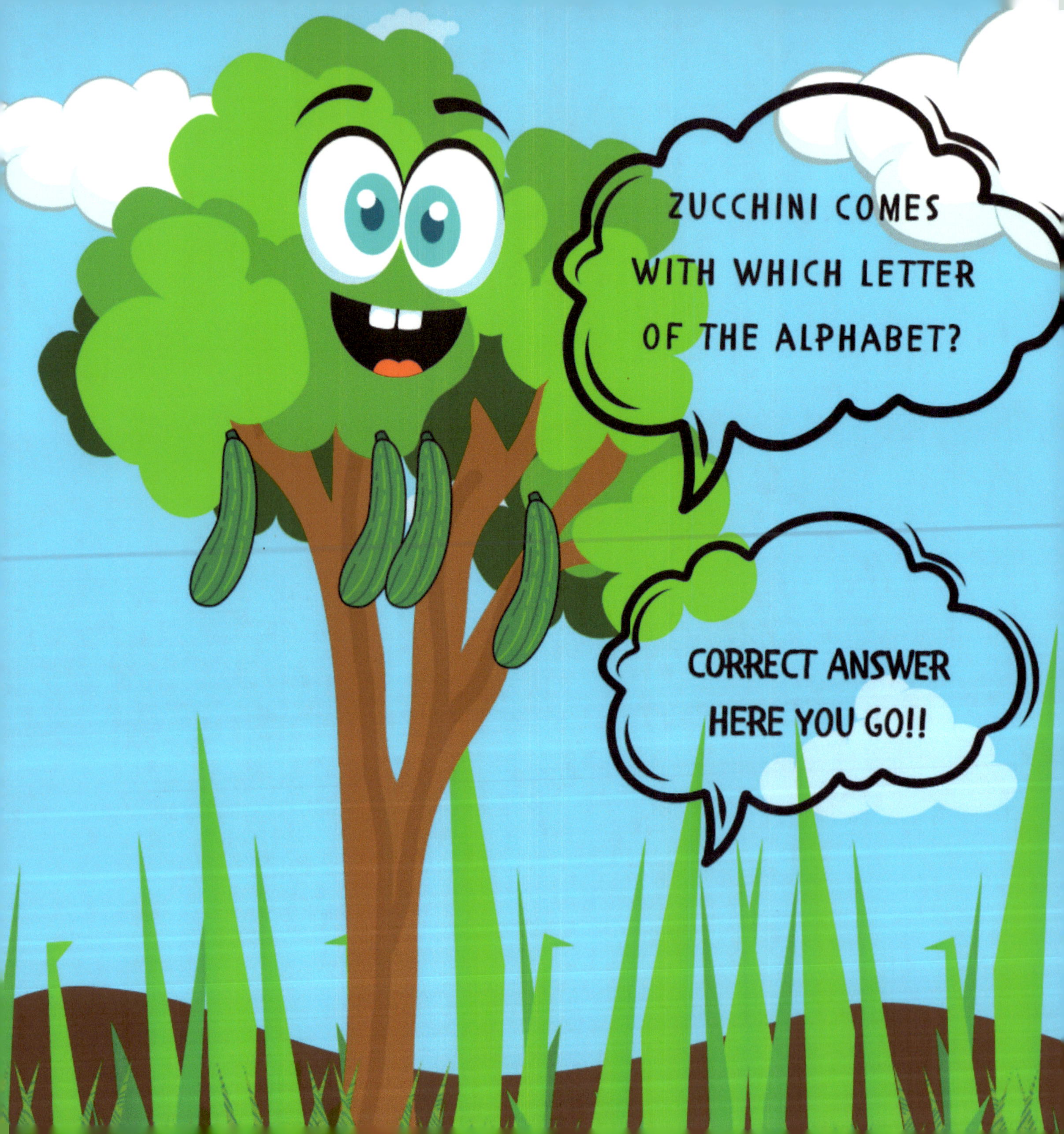

ZUCCHINI COMES WITH WHICH LETTER OF THE ALPHABET?
CORRECT ANSWER HERE YOU GO!!

HAPPY TREE !
HAPPY TREE !
I WANT ZUCCHINIS !
Z
FOR ZUCCHINI